Original title:
Whispers of the Sea

Copyright © 2025 Creative Arts Management OÜ
All rights reserved.

Author: Zachary Prescott
ISBN HARDBACK: 978-1-80581-522-8
ISBN PAPERBACK: 978-1-80581-049-0
ISBN EBOOK: 978-1-80581-522-8

Beneath the Ocean's Breath

Bubbles giggle, fish all play,
They tickle crabs in a silly way.
Starfish dance with a goofy glee,
Waving their arms like they're on a spree.

Seahorses race with a dainty prance,
While octopuses join in the dance.
A turtle sneezes, and laughter erupts,
As jellyfish jiggle and gently fluff.

Tales Carried by the Currents

A clam told a joke, the tide rolled in,
The sand dollar laughed, it's a victory win.
Anemones swayed with giddy delight,
While sandpipers cracked jokes from morning till night.

Lobsters wearing glasses, looking so fine,
Whispering secrets of oysters divine.
They gossip of treasures that lie way below,
While snails spin stories, all wrapped in a show.

Shadows of a Distant Horizon

Fish wearing hats? Oh what a sight!
Surfers all giggle when the waves take flight.
Crabs with a swagger, they walk on the sand,
While gulls tell tall tales, it's all quite unplanned.

The sunset's a canvas, colors collide,
With mermaids who chuckle as they take a ride.
A dolphin pops up, wearing glasses so round,
And joins in the fun, what a wacky sound!

Lullabies in the Foam

Pufferfish puff with a comical flair,
While the seaweed dances without a care.
Starfish snore loudly, under the sun,
As little crabs race, oh what a fun run!

The tides hum a tune, a wobbly beat,
With clownfish flipping, they're light on their feet.
Seashells join in with a rhythmic clap,
As the ocean sings softly, a bubbly rap.

Embrace of the Moonlit Waters

Bubbles rise and giggles spread,
A fish in a tux, dreams in its head.
Crabs moonwalk on the sandy floor,
While octopuses dance, what's in store?

Turtles wear shades, oh what a sight,
Seagulls argue, who's taking flight?
Jellyfish jive, feeling quite free,
Under the gaze of the moonlit sea.

Dreams in the Distant Surf

Waves crash in laughter, a frothy cheer,
Surfboards and seahorses, come have a beer!
Starfish sing ballads, off-key and loud,
While dolphins form a splashing crowd.

Sandcastles topple, a comedic scene,
As crabs pull pranks, oh what a routine!
Mermaids giggle, toss seaweed with glee,
Sandy shenanigans, just wait and see.

The Language of the Wind and Waves

The breeze tells jokes, tickling the shore,
Seagulls join in with a raucous roar.
Coconuts chuckle, rolling about,
As tides play tag, they're never in doubt.

Hermit crabs gossip, trading their shells,
While fish in bow ties pull off their spells.
Shells conspire over which one is best,
In this quirky realm, laughter's the quest.

Chants from the Abyss

Deep down, a grumpy old eel sings a tune,
His seaweed beard waving, oh what a swoon!
Clownfish comment with their colorful flair,
Underwater antics to lighten the air.

The bubble-blowing squid rehearses a play,
While bubbles pop, they scurry away.
Nemo's lost yet again, what a clout,
In the humor of depths, laughter's about.

Lonesome Lights on the Waterfront

A lighthouse stands with a grin,
Its flash says, "Come on in!"
Seagulls laugh at its bright show,
"No land here, just lots of glow!"

Fishing boats with silly names,
Bob around, playing their games.
One says, "Catch me if you can!"
While another sings of a tin can.

Echoes of the Past in the Salt Air

Old sailors tell tales of gold,
While their fishnets, bright and bold,
Dance around like fairies free,
"Have you seen the fish? Just me!"

Every wave a joke or two,
As crabs all dance in their own crew.
They pinch with laughter, don't you see?
Life's a party in salty glee.

The Shimmering Edge of Forever

The horizon winks, oh so sly,
"Catch a star, but don't ask why!"
Mermaids giggle, toss their hair,
"Who needs shoes? Just glide on air!"

Flip-flops fly and seagulls cheer,
"Let's create a splash, come near!"
The tide pulls back, then rushes in,
"Drenched again? You should wear skin!"

Messages Carried by the Waves

Bottles bob like disco balls,
Each filled with letters, funny calls.
A note inside says, "Send ice cream!"
Waves reply, "Now that's a dream!"

Surfboards slide with crazy flair,
While dolphins flip without a care.
"Life's a wave, just ride it right!"
And ocean frolics dance in sight.

Beneath Stars

Under the night, crabs dance in a line,
Telling jokes to the fish, all feeling just fine.
Stars wink above, like a cheeky light show,
Seagulls join in, with a comedic flow.

A starfish is giggling, tickled by sand,
While a whale sings high, like a rockstar band.
The moon starts to chuckle, casting its glow,
As laughter rolls in with the breezy flow.

Beneath Waters

Bubbles rise up, like laughter afloat,
A clam cracks a joke, oh what a great quote!
Fishes in suits, swimming with flair,
Tell tales of a shrimp that combed its fine hair.

Octopuses juggle with shells and great ease,
While turtles drop beats from the world's best CDs.
Coral reefs snicker, their colors so bright,
In this underwater circus, all's merry and light.

Murmurs of Forgotten Shores

On the beach, they gather, a sandy old crew,
With shells on their heads, and their laughter in view.
Seashells whisper secrets of the sand so grand,
While hermit crabs strut like they own this fine land.

A starfish tells riddles, to a crowd full of clams,
And gulls cackle loudly, drawing in all the jams.
The waves join the chorus, with their bubbly delight,
As the sun sets in gold, it's a comical sight.

Tales from the Tranquil Tide

Oh, what a sight, a fish in a hat,
Winks at a dolphin, who's fallen down flat.
With snickers in tide pools, the jellyfish swirl,
As a sea cucumber trips, it's a slippery whirl.

The tide rolls in with a giggling sound,
As sea urchins play pranks on the crabs all around.
Seaweed does a tango, swaying with cheer,
In this comical ballet, laughter's all you hear.

The Tide's Unseen Story

In the mist of the dawn, seashells convene,
Where the sand tickles toes, in this funny scene.
Mermaids share gossip, about splashing in waves,
While sea turtles whisper, of all the fun braves.

The tide pulls at socks, as it giggles away,
Seagulls plot mischief, they're in the fray.
It's a splash of pure joy with each rolling wave,
In this ocean of laughter, forever we crave.

The Enigmatic Breeze

A playful gust danced by my ear,
It whispered secrets, oh so clear.
Tales of fish in costume wear,
And crabs that boogie without a care.

The seagulls giggle, perched on high,
With jokes about the gullible pie.
My hat flew off, a chubby thief,
Now it's the ocean's new motif!

Breezes tickle all the sand,
While dolphins join the slapstick band.
Mermaids rolling, laughing loud,
In this salty, sunny crowd.

So come, my friend, let's catch a breeze,
And laugh till our worries take their leave.
For in the air, both light and free,
Lies the charm of the salty spree.

Dance of the Shells in the Wind

Shells do a jig on the golden shore,
Each rhyming step, a fabled lore.
One shell tripped and fell on its face,
While another wore sunglasses with grace.

Tide pools chuckle, with starfish cheer,
As crabs conduct a band without fear.
A conch horn blares, it's quite an act,
Who knew they were so shell-back intact?

Waves are laughing, rolling to and fro,
As sandy dancers join the show.
A waltz with a jellyfish, oh so bright,
Giggling as they sway in the light.

So gather 'round, don't miss the scene,
The beach is alive, with spirit and sheen.
For in this frolic, carefree and grand,
Life's a party on the shimmering sand.

The Soft Call of the Buoyant Horizon

The horizon giggles, a playful tease,
It calls out softly to the sailing breeze.
On boats with buoyancy—a jolly crew,
Waving at clouds that drip with dew.

Gulls swoop in, and they toss some fries,
Trading for laughter, oh what a prize!
Boats rock and waddle with glee so bright,
As fish wear hats and join the sight.

The sun starts to dance, round and fat,
Covered with sunscreen, just where it's at.
Nothing's serious under this bliss,
Even the dolphins swim to kiss!

So come along, enjoy the tide,
In this folly, let's take a ride.
For each wave carries a tickle and tease,
In the playful air that aims to please.

Remnants of the Siren's Song

Oh, that tune with a cheeky hum,
Echoes of laughter, oh what fun!
Sirens giggle on slippery rocks,
While wearing shells, they fool the clocks.

A tune that calls, but lures the wit,
Mermaids with jelly shoes, ready to flit.
"Come sing with us!" they sing with glee,
As they juggle fish in a raucous spree.

Tales of sailors lost in the jest,
Chasing the music, an endless quest.
Echoes of giggles float on the tide,
Creating a rhythm, with laughter as guide.

So heed the call, embrace the fun,
For beneath the waves, life's never done.
In this buoyant joke shared with flair,
The ocean chuckles, light as air.

Sighs of the Restless Waters

The waves are laughing, oh what a sight,
A crab wearing sunglasses, oh what a fright!
Fish in a conga, they dance 'neath the sun,
While gulls take a break, it's all just for fun.

Seagulls are shouting, got jokes to declare,
About mermaids drinking too much sea air.
A sea turtle grins, with a wink and a nod,
"Caught a wave on a dolphin, life's pretty odd!"

A starfish in slippers, he's ready to groove,
The ocean floor's moving, it's time to improve.
Coral's got drama, it's wild and it's free,
Underwater gossip, just wait and you'll see!

The tide breaks in chuckles, it's all quite absurd,
As otters engage in a game of word.
A clam tells his tales, just a bit of a tease,
In this world of water, no worries, just ease.

Chronicles of Celestial Seas

Bubbles pop laughter, a volcanic delight,
A pirate fish searching for treasure tonight.
Mermaids are pranking, their tails in a twist,
Flipping their fins, they can't resist!

The jellyfish jiggles, floats up to the beat,
Inventing new dance moves, isn't that neat?
While octopuses juggle their colorful loot,
Anemones cheer, it's the grandest hoot!

Starfish are gathering for an odd debate,
Who has the best style? It's never too late!
With flip-flopped opinions, they just can't agree,
As crabs roll their eyes, "Why can't we just be?"

In the shimmer and chaos, they thrive with great zest,
The quirkiest crew on this aquatic quest.
Upside down wonders in this whimsical show,
With giggles and splashes, let the fun flow!

Embrace of the Lapping Waves

Splash, giggle, and swish, the tide plays a game,
A dolphin pops up, as if to reclaim.
Seaweed's a wig that's oh-so chic,
The surfboards are laughing, they're never oblique!

Clams with the sass, they gossip and chat,
"Did you see that crab? He's gone really fat!"
A shrimp's on a mission to throw a grand feast,
But the sea cucumbers, they're never at least.

Whales sing in chorus, a comedic refrain,
With bubbles of humor, they share all the gain.
The tide tickles toes, what a lovely surprise,
As sea stars exchange their bright, sparkly ties!

The shore gets together for one last big show,
With laughter and splashes—a ceaseless flow.
Each perfect wave is a cheeky delight,
The ocean's a stage, where joy takes flight!

Surrender to the Blue

A dolphin danced with a goofy grin,
His flipper flapping like a silly fin.
The seabirds laughed, they all took flight,
While crabs did the cha-cha through the moonlight.

A seal with a hat sang a funny song,
The octopus juggled, it didn't take long.
As waves crashed down with a splashy cheer,
The whole ocean burst into laughter here!

Harmonies of the Coastline

A clam recited poetry with flair,
While the starfish sighed, 'This could be rare!'
As seaweed twirled with a graceful swoosh,
The waves whispered tales in the biggest whoosh.

A fish wore glasses, looked quite astute,
While a crab played guitar in a floral suit.
The tide brought in cheers, as shells all clapped,
In this coastal concert, no one was trapped!

Fables Flowing with the Ripples

Mermaids told jokes that left everyone giddy,
They swam in circles, their giggles quite witty.
An old turtle shared tales of a lost shoe,
While sea cucumbers giggled, 'Oh, what a view!'

The fish threw a party, with snacks from the brine,
A banquet of seaweed, oh, isn't it fine?
As barnacles danced on the ocean floor,
The whole sea laughed; who could ask for more?

Silence Heralded by the Sea

A crab on a throne took a regal pose,
Declared, 'All rise! Time for seaweed prose!'
While a fish dressed in stripes did a silly dance,
The sea swayed gently as if in a trance.

But laughter erupted; it echoed and roared,
As jellyfish spun, avoiding the bored.
In the calm of the night, the sea chose to sing,
Jokes about barnacles, oh what fun they bring!

Celestial Reflections in Tidepools

Tiny stars in puddles play,
The crabs perform their grand ballet.
Fishy faces, making silly grins,
Winking at the tide's wild spins.

Seaweed wigs on little fish,
Hopping high in water's swish.
All the sea is laughing loud,
With ripples dancing, oh so proud!

Jellyfish float like graceful clowns,
While starfish wear their best frowns.
Bubbles popping, what a treat,
Tickles from a crabby seat!

In these pools of shimmering glee,
The ocean's joke is plain to see.
So dive on in, take a look,
The jokes are here, just like a book!

The Dance of the Moonlit Waters

Under a moon that's far too bright,
The sea critters dance with delight.
A seagull sings off-key and loud,
The fish just laugh and form a crowd.

Mermaids giggle, twirling skirts,
While dolphins leap with silly flirts.
The waves roll in like playful pups,
Splashing the shore, filled with hiccups.

Stars winking down, they're in on the fun,
Keeping time to the splash and run.
Even the barnacles tap their feet,
To the beat of the rhythm, oh so sweet!

With a glimmer and a splash, we sway,
The ocean's party, come what may.
Join the fun, don't be a fool,
The water's got its own dance school!

Mysteries in the Foam

The foam rolls in with a silly grin,
It tickles toes and pulls you in.
What strange things hide in the white?
A rogue crab dancing, what a sight!

Salty secrets drift ashore,
A clam's first comedy encore.
With every wave, laughter grows,
Tip-toeing on slippery toes!

That barnacle with glasses thick,
Looks like he's up to some funny trick.
Shells holding tales of goofy fame,
All join in the sparkling game!

So let the bubbles speak their lore,
As creatures join the joyful roar.
Each frothy wave, a laugh to share,
In this foamy world, we lose all care!

Harmonies of Shells and Sand

On the shore where the shells do sing,
The crabs hold court, and seagulls swing.
Each grain of sand has a story to tell,
Of frogs in tuxedos, oh what the shell!

Bright colored shells all lined in rows,
Make a band of clattering bows.
They play a tune as the tide goes by,
With a little help from the breeze in the sky.

Sandcastles crumbling, but they don't mind,
They laugh and tumble, always kind.
Each wave a tune, a quirky jam,
With a twist, a turn, and a wiggly swam!

So bring your shells, let's start the show,
The beach is alive with a groovy flow.
Catch the fun in every grain,
In this dance of shells, we'll never wane!

Murmurs of the Ocean Depths

Bubbles rise like soda pop,
Fish play cards and never stop.
Crabs in tuxedos dance away,
While jellyfish float, sassy and gay.

Seashells gossip on the shore,
They tell tales of mermaids and more.
A clam with pearls takes center stage,
While seaweed laughs, a quirky sage.

Octopuses juggle, quite a sight,
With eight arms, they're always right.
Starfish cheer in the sandy seats,
As the tide rolls in with rhythmic beats.

Under waves, the laughter swells,
In this world, there are no spells.
Salty secrets fill the air,
Just sea creatures without a care.

The Language of Salt and Spray

Seagulls squawk like they own the place,
Sandy paws in a doggy race.
Surfboards laugh as they catch a wave,
While seashells plot how to behave.

A beach ball bounces, takes a dive,
Sandy toes each feel alive.
Bikini tops do the wiggly dance,
While the tide teases in a playful prance.

Nautical knick-knacks share a joke,
And dolphins giggle at the poke.
Waves invite the sun to play,
Making mischief in their own way.

Crabs build castles, quite the sight,
While starfish argue about what's right.
Together they form a seaside crew,
With laughter bursting, oh so true.

Songs Carried by the Wind

Kites fly high with squeaky sounds,
As whispers dance above the grounds.
Wind chimes laugh with rattle and sway,
While sandcastles yell, "Don't wash away!"

A dolphin winks, tips his hat,
As sea turtles practice their chat.
Mermaids giggling under the sun,
Call out, "Join us, come have fun!"

Waves surf the shores with a splashy quack,
Seashell bands play a lively track.
Crabs mc's with pinchers held high,
While gulls duet from the afternoon sky.

Breezy tunes wave all around,
As flip-flops dance without a sound.
Beach umbrellas keep secrets untold,
In this paradise, young and old.

Beneath the Coral Canopy

Corals gleam with colors so bright,
Fish throw parties late into night.
A clownfish cracks a funny line,
While anemones sway, looking divine.

Pufferfish puff, just for a laugh,
Octopus paints with flair, what a craft!
Clams of all kinds hold their shells, tight,
While seahorses tango, pure delight.

Tropical fish swim in jubilee,
Tickling each other with glee, you see.
Starfish wearing hats, oh what a sight,
Underwater fashion? Always tight.

Beneath the waves, the fun won't cease,
Every bubble bursts with joy and peace.
Coral castles rise like a dream,
In a world that sparkles and gleams.

Shadows on the Horizon

Out on the beach, a crab wore a hat,
He danced with the waves, said, 'How about that?'
A seagull squawked, stealing snacks in flight,
While fish were gossiping, things got tight.

The tide came in, and so did the fun,
Starfish on parade, the sun had begun.
Shells rolled their eyes, said, 'What a show!'
While dolphins cracked jokes, swimming to and fro.

A sandcastle stood, wearing a crown,
But the tide said, 'Nope,' and it washed it down.
Lighthouses grinned, gave a flickering wink,
'We see all the chaos, what do you think?'

So next time you wander on that sandy shore,
Look for the humor, there's always more.
Picnic with laughter, the ocean's sweet tease,
Life is a party, if you just let it please.

The Call of Distant Shores

A clam held a concert, what a weird sight!
With barnacles bobbing, they partied all night.
The tide rolled in, bringing old fish tales,
Lobsters were laughing, creating a scale.

The mermaids joined in, singing a tune,
While seahorses twirled under the light of the moon.
Starfish played cards, betting with clams,
While the octopus juggled his slew of jams.

A surfer yelled, 'Hey, I caught a big wave!'
It turned out to be a curious knave.
With seaweed as garments, they danced 'til the dawn,
And washed up together, none could be drawn.

So if you're near waves with a smile on your face,
Know that the ocean is a comedic place.
Each splash and each bubble, a joke on the floor,
Where laughter and currents forever explore.

Lullabies from the Abyss

In the deep blue, a whale hums to a tune,
While squids practice tango, under the moon.
The jellyfish giggle, glowing like stars,
Bubbles burst loudly, "Let's see who's the czar!"

Fish gather 'round, with a soft little cheer,
'Hey, octopus, show us your best career!'
He juggled some shells with style and flair,
While eel shook its tail, as if to declare.

A crab told a tale of a pirate's dread,
Who lost his gold doubloons in the seaweed bed.
With a splash and a dance, they forgot their woes,
In the calm watery world, where joy freely flows.

So when life gets heavy, take a dip and see,
The absurdity thriving underneath the sea.
There's fun in the depths, with tales to impress,
Join the laughing marine, for it's bound to bless.

Currents of Silent Stories

In the harbor, a fish shared a secret idea,
To swap out their fins for some stylish new gear.
Clams tried on glasses, all the rage at the shore,
While snails slapped high-fives, wanting just more.

The boats bobbed gently, giggling with glee,
Saying, 'Look at us! Who has the best spree?'
The gulls on the roof were making remarks,
'Those waves are making us kings, little sparks!'

The water was bubbling, laughter out loud,
As the funny old crab led a whimsical crowd.
With nets full of nonsense, they danced in delight,
Making memories sweet as the stars spark bright.

So let your heart wander where the laughter flows,
And follow the currents where humor bestows.
For life's a big ocean, where tales intertwine,
Catch the joy in the waves, let your spirit shine.

Mists Over Forgotten Waters

In the fog, a crab does dance,
Wearing goggles, taking a chance.
Fish below in a silly race,
Bubble trouble, what a place!

Seagulls squawk in vibrant hues,
Stealing chips and singing blues.
A mermaid spills her scented oils,
On a sailor with fishy spoils.

Jellyfish float like clowns in flight,
Tickling toes in the pale moonlight.
With a splash, a dolphin grins,
Playing tag where the surf begins.

So come enjoy the salty air,
With laughter, we'll shed every care.
In this mist, let's find our cheer,
Through giggles brought by ocean's sneer.

Songs of the Tidal Wanderer

A seagull sings a catchy tune,
Riding waves beneath the moon.
Sandcastles crumble with a splash,
As tides giggle, making a dash.

A fish with shades, he swims in style,
Winking at folks with a cheeky smile.
While crabs become the dance floor kings,
Clacking claws to the music that clings.

The tide does jiggle, a lively show,
With starfish spinning in the flow.
Octopuses juggle seashells with flair,
While sea cucumbers just don't care!

So listen close to the coastal beat,
Where laughter and waves meet, oh so sweet.
In this world of frolic and play,
Join the fun, don't be shy—come stay!

Echoing Lullabies of the Coast

Under stars, the tide hums low,
With echoes of tales from long ago.
A whale calls out with a boisterous sneeze,
Sending fish into fits—what a tease!

Saltwater tickles the toes of night,
As snails race slow in lantern light.
The crabs are plotting a sneaky heist,
But end up caught in a clam's paradise.

Seashells chime like bells on strings,
As sea urchins fashion tiny rings.
A starfish dreams of conquering lands,
While jellyfish float with graceful hands.

So lay down here on the sandy shore,
Where laughter's soft and the waves roar.
These echoes of fun will pull you near,
Chasing giggles as we sing and cheer.

Harmony of the Rolling Swells

On rolling swells, the turtles sway,
Grooving slowly, come join the play.
Seaweed dancers in vibrant green,
Twirl and twist, they're quite the scene!

A pirate parrot squawks out loud,
As dolphins leap and gather a crowd.
With a flip and a splash, they steal the show,
Cracking jokes, oh what a flow!

A clam in shells sits snug and tight,
Dreaming of jelly at the sandy night.
While fish in bow ties strut with pride,
Beneath the waves, where giggles abide.

Come take a ride on this joyous crest,
Where laughter dances and never rests.
In this realm of rolling glee,
Let's sing and laugh by the azure sea!

Tides of Silent Secrets

The crab wore a tie, just to impress,
Seaweed danced wildly in a humorous mess.
Fish knitted a sweater for the old blue whale,
He swam in circles, always on the trail.

Octopus threw a party, bubbles did fly,
Jellyfish jelly, spread on toast, oh my!
Starfish played poker, bluffing with glee,
"Anyone for a game?" said the plankton with a spree.

Barnacles giggled, clinging so tight,
A clam told a joke that gave fish a fright.
"Why did the sea sponge fail his exam?"
"Because he didn't study, he just went 'blam!'"

In the end, they laughed at the moon's soft glow,
While the tide came in, stealing the show.
Secrets exchanged in the cool ocean foam,
An underwater circus, a frolicsome home.

Echoes Beneath the Waves

A dolphin in shades is swimming on by,
Says, "Why don't fish play cards? They're afraid to try!"
Eels tangled in seaweed, making a fuss,
"Can someone untangle us? This is a bus!"

Seahorses galloped, what a sight to behold,
With shells as their tickets, they were mighty bold.
"Next stop, the reef!" shouted Captain Clam,
"Bring your best jokes, I've got a jam!"

Turtles twirled in pairs, doing the twist,
Land crabs joined in, they couldn't resist.
"Who's got the best dance? It's a fierce little race,"
But a wave crashed in, splashing foam on their face.

The echo of laughter rolled under the swell,
As creatures recounted their tales to tell.
With bubbles and giggles, they played till the night,
Under a blanket of stars, what a delight!

Murmurs of the Deep

The anglerfish grinned with a glow up front,
"Let's lighten the mood; let's have some fun!"
Whales sang songs that tickled the deep,
While squids threw confetti, and fish danced in leaps.

A wave rolled in, with a splash of surprise,
Mollusks wore sunglasses, oh, what a prize!
"Join us, dear clownfish, don't hang by the reef,"
They laughed as he spluttered, "I'm a little too chief!"

Crabs cracked some puns, causing quite the stir,
"Why did the guppy get a bicycle spur?"
"Because it was tired of just going in circles,"
Then danced to the rhythm, all fish in the circles.

The murmur grew loud, a symphony bright,
As creatures shared jokes under soft moonlight.
With every splash, the ocean grew bold,
In stories and laughter, the deep became gold.

Songs from the Sandy Shore

The seagulls squawked a catchy refrain,
'Oh, what a day, let's dance in the rain!'
With shells as maracas, they shook to the beat,
As sand crabs tap danced on their tiny little feet.

A clam and a shrimp formed a duo so sweet,
They sang of adventures and clam chowder treat.
"Why is the sand cold? It's got no warm shoes,"
The audience roared, "Such amusing excuses!"

Tides rolled in with a slap and a tickle,
"Hey, sea stars, come join, we've got quite the pickle!"
Sands had a talent show, laughter would soar,
As they showcased their acts on the golden sea floor.

As the sun dipped down, painting skies bright,
The songs from the shore filled the warm night.
With giggles and chuckles, they bid adieu,
In the sea's endless humor, they found something true.

Secrets in the Salt

The fish gathered round for a chat,
Discussing the best place to splat.
They giggled and wobbled, quite out of tune,
Wondering if seaweed could make for a boon.

A crab in a bow tie offered a joke,
He chuckled so hard, he nearly bespoke.
"Why don't we play hide and seek with the waves?
Because the last time we drowned, it was just misbehaves!"

The sea cucumbers danced with delight,
While the lobsters turned red, quite a sight.
The starfish gave high fives to the sand,
Mirth dripped like water, oh wasn't it grand!

So if you ever feel blue on the shore,
Just listen for laughter, there's always more.
In this world of salt, where silliness thrives,
The ocean's a party; it's where fun survives!

The Call of the Shells

A clam shouted loud, "It's a shell-a-bration!"
Echoing through tides with much adulation.
The conch blew a tune full of sass,
While the mussels just laughed, joining the class.

The oysters held court with pearls to declare,
Like royalty, they posed without a care.
"Who needs a crown when you're shiny and slick?
Join us for treasure; it's just like a trick!"

Tiny snails crawled in a race so slow,
As the hermit crabs cheered for their glow.
"On your mark, get set, let's leave behind trails,
As we search the beach for humorous tales!"

With laughter like bubbles, they rolled on the shore,
Shells stacked as trophies—who could want more?
In this salty place, every shell holds a jest,
So come dive right in; it's a shell of a fest!

Gentle Voices of the Tide

The tide rolled in like a jolly old friend,
Gurgling stories that seemed to blend.
"Do you hear that?" said the seagull with glee,
"It's a tale of a fish who forgot to flee!"

A sea sponge chimed in with a giggle so bright,
"I once had a nightmare that I'd be tonight's bite!"
The waves crashed with laughter, a bubbly cheer,
As the jellyfish danced, fluttering near.

Starfish twirled tales on the soft sandy floor,
Teasing the barnacles stuck to the shore.
"Life is a hoot; let's swim and proclaim,
Every splash brings a grin, not just any old name!"

So if you're feeling dull by the briny expanse,
Just listen for chuckles; join in the dance.
For here in the currents, fun is a tide,
Where even the waves love to take you for a ride!

Reflections on an Indigo Surface

On indigo waves, the sun takes a bow,
As quirky fish ponder, "Just where are we now?"
"Are we swimming in circles or just taking the day?
Let's just keep moving; it's all just a play!"

A dolphin leapt high, slipping over the crest,
With a flip and a wink, he declared, "I'm the best!"
The octopus chuckled, "That's quite a splash,
I've got eight great moves, can you match my dash?"

The reflections would giggle, buoyed by the fun,
As crabs on the rocks shouted, "Who's not yet done?"
With laughter and bubbles filling the air,
The ocean's a circus, with antics to share!

So next time you gaze at the blue, wide expanse,
Remember the joy and take a chance.
For in the great waters, with each little squirt,
There lies a deep humor, and oh, how it flirts!

Currents of Solitude

A crab on the beach with a very strange hat,
Said to a seagull, "You're looking quite fat!"
The waves laughed aloud, with a bubbly cheer,
As a fish flipped and flopped, saying, "What's that gear?"

A clam tried to sing, but it sounded like snore,
The jellyfish danced, saying, "I can do more!"
With shells as their instruments, they formed a grand band,
But a starfish just sat, giving sand a thumbs up hand.

A dolphin named Larry thought he'd tell a joke,
But all that came out was a loud, goofy croak!
The tides rolled in laughter, causing quite a ruckus,
As the ocean's humor left everyone flustered.

In solitude swimming, they found joy instead,
Silly little creatures, with laughter widespread.
The moonlight cast shadows on sand's soft embrace,
Where even the barnacles stuck out their face.

Rhythms of the Ebb and Flow

The tide rolls in with a giggle and gleam,
While a crab played the drums, living out its dream.
A whale shared a pun that made everyone squeal,
And the rays spun around like a goofy old wheel.

As waves take a bow, the sea turtles roll,
Attempting some dancing, but losing control.
Each splash told a tale, with laughter galore,
While an octopus juggled and begged for an encore.

"Hey fish!" shouted Sally, with a wave of her fin,
"Let's throw a big party, let the fun begin!"
With snickers and bubbles, the ocean took flight,
As currents of humor brought pure delight.

From clams with their quirks, to squids with their tricks,
Every creature swayed to the rhythms that mix.
In the ebb and the flow, each moment a jest,
Where laughter was cherished, and joy truly blessed.

Voices Lost to the Wind

A parrot named Pete thought he could croon,
But all that came out sounded like a cartoon.
The gulls rolled their eyes, with a sarcastic squawk,
As they strutted along, cracking jokes on the dock.

A starfish declared, "I'll show you a dance!"
But with no legs to move, it failed at its chance.
The crabs formed a circle, with claws in the air,
While the anchovies giggled, quite happy to share.

The dolphins would dive, and they'd spin in the brine,
Making waves of laughter, feeling just so fine.
With fish that would flop and seagulls that chase,
No one could deny it, their antics embraced.

Lost voices of mirth, tucked in each nook,
The ocean's a stage, with a storybook hook.
Amongst windswept whispers, the fun can't be drowned,
In a watery world where joy can be found.

The Dusk that Keeps its Secrets

As the sun dips low in a bright orange glow,
A clam tried to whisper secrets from below.
The gulls gathered round, eager to hear,
But all they could catch was a loud salty sneer.

The tide chuckled softly at the stories amiss,
While a squid wrote a novel—no ending, just bliss.
A fish stole the script, said, "I'm the main star!"
And the ocean erupted in laughter from far.

With shadows that danced, and foam in a swirl,
The secrets of dusk made each fish do a twirl.
They splashed and they played, with jests flying free,
In a world filled with giggles, just wait till you see!

As starlight came out, the giggles grew bold,
The ocean spilled secrets that never grow old.
In the still of the night, with humor its guide,
The sea held its laughter, a joyful wild ride.

Tales of the Brooding Gulls

Up at dawn, the gulls convene,
With a squawking team, quite the scene.
They squabble for chips, it's quite a fuss,
Like a beachside brawl, they'll make a fuss.

One steals a fry, oh what a plot!
Another dives in, they're fighting a lot.
With feathers flying, they pirouette,
It's avian drama, no sign of regret.

When high tides call, they soar and play,
Actor or seagull? Who's won today?
Their antics make folks laugh and grin,
These feathered jesters, with chaos within.

And as night falls, they take a break,
Dreaming of fries, for goodness' sakes!
In the salty breeze, their laughter will ring,
These brooding gulls, the pranksters of spring.

Ciphers of the Rushing Waves

The waves come in with a bubbly cheer,
A frothy tangle, oh dear oh dear!
They tickle the toes and crash on the shore,
A playful dance, they yearn for more.

Bubbles gurgle secrets, they can't quite share,
Like fishy gossip floating through air.
They tease the beachgoers, splash with glee,
"Dare you to catch us, oh can't you see?"

A flip-flop lost, oh what a sight,
A wave just chuckled, "I did it right!"
They whisper of silly, but none can decode,
This riddle of waters, their watery ode.

Yet amidst the fun, a shell takes a stand,
"Stop laughing now, this is my land!"
But laughter prevails as the tide flows free,
With the waves as jesters, who'd disagree?

The Sea's Heartbeat

A lullaby hums from depths below,
Crabs tap dance in a rhythmic show.
The tide rolls out, then pulls back in,
With a splashy giggle, the fun begins.

Starfish lounge, wearing shades of lime,
They sunbathe, basking without a time.
"Hey there, fish, can you do the twist?"
In the watery world, nobody's missed.

Seaweed flutters, waving with flair,
"Join our party, if you dare!"
They boogie down under, oh what a blast,
In the aquatic rave, the fun is vast.

And when night falls, the dolphins leap,
With a wink and a grin, their secrets they keep.
A splash in the dark, with giggles that glide,
In this lively ocean, let the fun ride.

Echoes of Ancient Mariners

Old ships creak with a voice of lore,
Sailing tales of mischief, legends of yore.
"Ho ho ho!" they laugh in the dark,
With stubborn barnacles, a nautical spark.

The captain once tripped on his own two feet,
"Beware the plank!" he'd yell with a beat.
But the crew just chuckled and danced on the deck,
As the gulls swooped low, making quite the wreck.

"Set the sails! Or maybe not,"
"Let's have a party, you sea-bound lot!"
With barrels of grog and fishy delight,
Their echoes still linger on moonlit nights.

So raise a toast to the seafaring bands,
With pirate hats and squishy rubber bands.
In echoes of old, laughter still sails,
On the backs of the waves, where adventure prevails.

Memories Etched in Seashells

In tides that tease and flirt with sand,
Seashells laughing, a silly band.
They trade their tales with a sassy glee,
As crabs strut past, quite fancy-free.

A starfish winks from behind a rock,
Says, "Keep it down, don't mock my clock!"
The ocean's lull, a giggle and cheer,
Makes every splash a laugh to hear.

Fish with hats dance in the swell,
Singing songs they know too well.
With every ripple, a ticklish plot,
Creating joy at the very spot.

Oysters snicker, pearls in tow,
As minnows play peek-a-boo, you know.
A world so bright, with laughter to fill,
Seashells and secrets, always a thrill.

Celestial Dance of the Ocean

The moon's a dancer, swirling bright,
In a tutu made of silver light.
Stars giggle as they sway in time,
With waves that bubble up in rhyme.

Fish wear shades and strut their stuff,
Saying, "Come on, this isn't tough!"
Dolphins jump, all smiles and flair,
Making waves with a splash and air.

Crabs throw a party on the shore,
With conch shells beating, hear them roar!
As seagulls dive for a snack or two,
They join the fun, now how about you?

The tides bring humor, a playful tease,
With every splash, a gentle breeze.
This cosmic scene in nature's plot,
Will tickle your soul, like it or not.

Soft Glimmers on the Water's Edge

Sun-kissed beams tramp on the coast,
Jellyfish giggle, they're the most!
They sway like dancers, all floppy and free,
Inviting laughter from you and me.

Seagulls squawk a silly tune,
Dropping fries like a cartoon.
They steal a sandwich, then take flight,
Causing chaos, oh what a sight!

Buckets and spades ready for play,
Building castles that melt away.
Sand crabs peek, curious eyes aglow,
As kids squeal, "Where'd our tower go?"

The shoreline giggles, a comedic spree,
Nature's jesters, wild and free.
In this world where laughter flows,
Every glance brings a chuckle that grows.

Beacons of the Coastal Night

The lighthouse beams, a cheeky grin,
While waves play tag, a game to win.
With each flicker, the seagulls dive,
In a quest for snacks, they come alive!

Stars compete in a twinkling race,
With constellations all in place.
"Catch me if you can!" they tease the tide,
As dolphins giggle, they take a ride.

Shells gossip softly, secrets in tow,
As crabs perform their nightly show.
With every clap from the happy crowd,
The coastal night's joy is loud and proud.

So come along, let your spirits be light,
Join the frolic through the starry night.
With every wave, a chuckle's found,
In this silly symphony, we're all spellbound.

A Symphony Under the Stars

The fish hold concerts, oh what a sight,
With scales like confetti, they dance through the night.
Crabs in tuxedos, they clap and they cheer,
While octopuses juggle, let's all give a sneer.

Seagulls are joining, with tunes that are flat,
Singing about lunch, and donning a hat.
The tide rolls in, like a chorus in queue,
Just watch where you step, there's seaweed for you!

The starfish are lounging, all lazy and round,
As jellyfish twirl, with grace that astounds.
A show like no other, beneath the starlight,
Where laughter and bubbles blend into the night.

So come hear the echoes of nature's own band,
Where every little creature has its own planned stand.
From barnacles rapping, to clams doing a jig,
In this grand ocean symphony, life's never too big.

Mirage of the Endless Blue

A dolphin named Dave, with a penchant for tricks,
Tries to surf the waves, but just ends up in fix.
He flips and he flops, like he's lost in a game,
The fish all laugh wildly, but he stays the same.

The turtles are sunbathing, lost in their dreams,
While seaweed does waltzes, or so it seems.
A mermaid named Claire, with hair made of foam,
Claims she once dated, a clam from the dome.

Seagulls poke fun, with their raucous old calls,
Making up stories of fish in the stalls.
Bubbles rise up, like laughter in air,
In this funny seaside, there's joy everywhere!

The sand crabs hold meetings, about who's the best,
While oysters play poker, with pearls in their chest.
A mirage in the blue, where laughter runs free,
Come join this fish party, it's all about glee!

Tides of Echoing Dreams

The waves are gossiping, with tales of the night,
Of sharks that wear glasses and fish that take flight.
A starfish named Stan, in the big ocean's cheer,
Swears he once danced with a whale at a fair.

The clownfish are laughing, with colors so bright,
Making silly faces, and causing a fright.
They juggle their seaweed, and puff up their cheeks,
In the tides of their dreams, hilarity peaks.

The eels do a tango, all slippery and spry,
While seahorses prance, giving twirls as they fly.
Hermit crabs shuffle, in their little round homes,
While fishy comedians crack jokes as they comb.

So ride on the waves, where the humor is thick,
With laughter like bubbles, that'll make you all tick.
In the tides of your dreams, let the fun never cease,
For the ocean's a place where joy finds its peace.

Secrets Beneath the Waves

Beneath the blue surface, secrets unfold,
Of turtles who gossip and stories retold.
A mollusk named Gary, claims he's quite wise,
But all he does is wear seaweed disguise.

The fish hold debates, about who swims the best,
While barnacles cling, taking each day as a quest.
A crab in a crown holds a court under swells,
And announces new laws for the fish with loud bells!

The sea cucumbers still just sit there all day,
Yet their gossip is golden, in quite a sly way.
Their wisdom comes slow, like the tide from afar,
But when they do speak, it's like "wow, what a star!"

So dive into the splash, where the secrets take flight,
And dance with the waves that glisten in light.
For beneath all the blues, where the bubbles are born,
Lies a tale of laughter, from dusk until dawn.

Nature's Silent Soliloquy

The crab does a jig on the shore,
With sideways steps, he craves for more.
A seagull squawks, 'Hey, that's my treat!'
As fish slip by, they're quick on their feet.

The tide pulls back, a sneaky prank,
Shells hide in sand, a crafty bank.
Laughter bubbles from waves that crash,
While starfish lounge, they giggle in a flash.

Seaweed dances, a green ballet,
As little fish ask, 'Can we join play?'
A lone sand dollar, proud and round,
Claims he's the king, but can't make a sound.

Octopus winks with colors bright,
Blending in, he's quite the sight.
A treasure chest, with dreams untold,
Hides jokes and giggles, the ocean's gold.

The Soft Breath of Ocean Breezes

The breezes carry stories old,
Of pirate tales and treasure gold.
A clam sits proud, a pearl in tow,
Sassier than most, 'Look at me glow!'

Seashells play hide and seek in sand,
Each one hoping to meet a hand.
Fish with sunglasses swim by with flair,
Saying, 'We're cool, just breathe the air.'

Bubbles rise like jokes in the mist,
While dolphins jump and twist with a twist.
The sun sets low, a golden ball,
And evening calls, 'Time for a ball!'

Crabs dig in for a nighttime snack,
While waves tickle toes, 'Hey, come back!'
The breeze whispers soft, sweet dreams to keep,
As the ocean laughs and lulls to sleep.

A Tidal Serenade

The waves sing tunes in a bubbly voice,
While fish do flips, they rejoice.
A jellyfish wobbles, a floaty sight,
Says, 'Join my dance, it's pure delight!'

Tide pools giggle with creatures small,
As crabs tap dance, giving a call.
A sea star spreads its arms so wide,
Claiming, 'I'm the best, no need to hide!'

The moon peeks down, a silvery grin,
As otters play, their games begin.
They slide on rocks and make quite a mess,
'We're just testing this, we must confess!'

Gulls squawk in rhythm, a funny choir,
Their off-key calls spark laughter's fire.
Each wave a jest, each breeze a pun,
In the ocean's frolic, we find our fun.

Veils of Mist at Dawn

The morning fog rolls in like a cloak,
Hiding sea turtles who giggle and poke.
They peek from shadows with a sly little grin,
As fish in schools make a splashy spin.

The seagulls gossip, 'Did you hear the news?'
About a crab wearing bright pink shoes.
He struts on the beach, with style and grace,
Chasing seagulls at a comical pace.

A lighthouse yawns, blinking with glee,
While boats bob up and down with me.
The tides play tricks, a fickle friend,
Shy or bold, it's all just pretend.

As the sun peeks out with a warm embrace,
Oceans chuckle, 'Welcome to our space!'
In misty veils, the day finds its cheer,
With laughter afloat, the coast is clear!

The Ancestral Waves Speak

The waves have tales of fishy lore,
Of mermaids, sailors, and the ocean's roar.
They gossip of treasures lost in the deep,
And crabby secrets that they keep.

With each splash, they tickle the shore,
While seagulls squawk, demanding more.
As sandcastles crumble, they laugh and tease,
Just trying to catch a floating breeze.

Bubbles bubble with laughter bright,
As ocean foam dances in the light.
The sea's a jokester, playful and spry,
Always ready for a salty reply.

So listen closely, next time you roam,
The waves are sharing tales from their foam.
Between the tides and the rolling spray,
You'll find their humor in a splashy way.

Shadows of the Lighthouse

The lighthouse keeper forgot to eat,
Thinking his role was to simply greet.
His shadow dances with ocean's grin,
While barnacles giggle, 'Oh, where's he been?'

He'll flick the light for passing ships,
But sometimes dreams of fishy trips.
With every beacon, a chuckle escapes,
As shadows shift in funny shapes.

The gulls make faces, mocking his style,
As he adjusts his glasses, aloof and fragile.
Peering wide, he spots them all,
A fishy gang that made his fall.

Through wind and waves, his duties bear,
Yet laughter lingers in the salty air.
For every storm that shakes his place,
He finds humor in the lighthouse race.

Shores Adrift in Memory

On sandy shores where socks get lost,
And flip-flops dance, no matter the cost.
The tide comes in with a silly grin,
Stealing our snacks, oh, where to begin?

Kids dig deep, looking for gold,
But find only shells with stories told.
Each wave that crashes, a riddle thrown,
Of sticky ice cream cones that have blown.

The beach ball bounces, a game gone awry,
While seagulls laugh as they swoop and fly.
With every crash of the frothy tide,
Memories of laughter are rolled aside.

So grab your bucket, let's make a splash,
In the joy of the ocean, where smiles are brash.
On shores that whisper secrets so sweet,
In every grain, our laughter repeats.

Interludes with the Sirens

The sirens sing, with voices so bright,
Offering fish sticks late in the night.
With hair made of kelp and eyes full of glee,
They lure unsuspecting sailors by the tree.

But lo and behold, it's just a grand ruse,
They serve up seaweed like it's fine stew.
With giggles and winks, they dance on the waves,
Tricking the sailors like mischievous knaves.

"Oh come join us, let's frolic and play,
We've got jellyfish for lunch today!"
But when the sailors meet their gaze,
They find it's all just a salty phase.

Yet tales of their antics float near and far,
The sirens' laughter shines like a star.
So beware the song that calls you in,
For laughter and fish sticks, they'll surely win.

Celestial Currents and Earthly Ties

A fish wore a hat quite askew,
He claimed it was all the rage, too.
In currents so grand, they'd laugh and dance,
While crabs did a jig in the moonlight's trance.

The octopus painted a canvas bright,
With seaweed strands—a curious sight.
The starfish, a critic, waved a fine limb,
"Darling, those colors are far too dim!"

Dolphins debated the latest ocean news,
"Did you hear about Sally? She's lost her shoes!"
They flipped and they flopped, what a ruckus they made,
With schools of sardines joining the parade.

"Let's throw a ball!" a clam called out loud,
So they danced 'neath the waves with a seawater crowd.
Each splash was a giggle, a playful delight,
In the world beneath waves, laughter took flight.

Driftwood Narratives

A piece of driftwood with stories to tell,
Sat watching the waves, casting its spell.
"Once I was part of a grand sailing ship,
Now I'm a throne for a crab, what a trip!"

Barnacles gathered, a gossiping crew,
"Did you hear about Sandy? She's turning quite blue!"
With tales of old anchors and sunken gold,
They shared tales of treasure in grand currents bold.

A jellyfish passed with a glimmering glee,
"It's all about style; just look at me!"
While seagulls above squabbled over a fry,
The driftwood just sighed, "Oh my, oh my!"

So they laughed till it echoed across the tide,
In the land of the silly, they let joy reside.
Though life may be tough on the water's crest,
Together, they knew they were truly blessed.

When Oceans Speak to the Moon

The tides tossed about on a high-spirited spree,
As waves made calls to the moon with glee.
"Hey Luna, you lovely, round ball of delight,
Come join our splash party, it's out of sight!"

In the water, it twinkled, a dazzling dance,
While clams hatched plans with a mischievous glance.
"The more you shine, the more we'll play!"
As they twirled through the foam, in their usual way.

Yet the moon just chuckled, in silver and glow,
"I'm busy with craters, can't come down below."
But tides kept on trying, with splashes and spray,
"Let's make a wave, let's surf the Milky Way!"

So laughter erupted from deep ocean floors,
As fish wore sunglasses and opened some doors.
In their frolicking fun, they forgot the tide's tale,
Just a night full of joy in a shimmering veil.

The Echoing Lure of the Current

The current was cheeky, a rascal at heart,
Bidding fish to follow and playfully dart.
"C'mon folks, it's a ride without fear,
Where oil spills are jokes, and the krill bring the cheer!"

A dolphin called out, "This is quite the thrill,
Last week I found treasure, a bright shiny hill!"
With tails all a-wagging, they spun round and round,
While the stubborn old turtle just grumbled and frowned.

"Back in my day, we swam with such grace,
Now it's all selfies and seaworthy race!"
But the crew just ignored him, too busy to mind,
In their whirl of adventures, that grump was left behind.

So the current kept teasing, with splashes of fun,
Where laughter and bubbles were never outdone.
In the ocean's grand tapestry, joy wasn't shy,
Just a playful parade beneath the bright sky!

www.ingramcontent.com/pod-product-compliance
Lightning Source LLC
Chambersburg PA
CBHW072133070526
44585CB00016B/1657